©2018 Mary J. Bryant, author

Kingdom Builders Publications, LLC

D. Yvonne N. Means, editor

Eric Quzack, illustrator

This Book Belongs to

Dedication

This book is dedicated to Marquis (pronounced Mar-kiss) Jarod Bryant, our youngest son, who is the inspiration for The Marquis Adventures series.

Lately, Marquis had been putting away his toys, eating his vegetables, brushing his teeth, and washing behind his ears. Marquis' mother was so impressed that she decided to take him to the circus.

"Marquis, I am so proud of you!" she exclaimed. "I knew you could do it because you are a big boy. I believe you deserve a treat."

Marquis began to jump up and down. He asked excitedly, "What mom? What will you give me?"

She thought for a moment. "Umm, let's see. What will that treat be?" Marquis waited in great suspense with his eyes wider than a quarter.

"I know. I am going to take you to the circus," his mother said.

"Oh yes!" clapped Marquis. "I love going to the circus to see all the animals. The elephants are my favorite. I would like to ride on an elephant one day."

Marquis was so excited that his mom had to calm him down. "Now, now Little Man, let's calm down a little. I don't think it's a good idea for you to ride on an elephant."

"But why not, mom? I have been eating my vegetables; and I am big and strong," he said as he showed off his muscles.

Marquis' mother patted him on the head and gave him a gentle smile. "Yes, you are big and strong, Marquis."

"I also like the clowns. Maybe I can take a picture with one of the clowns," Marquis said.

"We will see Marquis, but don't get your hopes up," she said.

The circus was coming to town in a week. Marquis' mother bought the tickets and they were all set to go. Soon it was time to go to the circus. Marquis reminded her to get the camera to take pictures.

"Let's get in the car!" Marquis said while running to get in the back seat.

"Don't forget to buckle up Little Man." she said.

"Oops! I was so excited, I almost forgot to buckle up, but I'm buckled up now mom!" Marquis exclaimed.

Before long, they arrived at the circus. Marquis was so very excited. He skipped all the way to the entrance. His mom gave the ticket taker their tickets and Marquis was given a pass to meet some of the circus members. What a surprise that was for him. She arranged for him to meet the clowns before the show started.

The first clown Marquis met was named Chico. Chico was a happy clown. He shook Marquis' hand and said "Hello little one. What is your name?"

Marquis looked up at him and said, "My name is Marquis, but my mom calls me Little Man sometimes."

Chico said, "Please to meet you Little Man. Do you want to take a picture with me?"

"Oh boy!" Marquis yelled as he asked his mother to help him take a selfie with Chico. Chico and Marquis posed for their picture.

"Thank you so very much Mr. Chico!" Marquis exclaimed.

They moved on to the next clown. He was blowing up balloons that were different colors. Some were filled with air, some were filled with water, and some were filled with toys. They were for the show.

"Well, who do we have here?" asked another clown.

"My name is Marquis." he smiled. "What's your name Mr. Clown?"

"Well, you can call me Trickster!" danced the clown.

"What are you going to do with all those balloons?" asked Marquis.

"It is a surprise and I can't tell you yet." Trickster said.

Marquis made a sad face. Trickster said, "Don't be sad. What if I get you to help me with my balloon trick?"

Marquis' frown turned upside down.

"Oh boy! May I mom, may I? Please?"

"Yes, you may," his mom agreed.

Trickster said he would come for Marquis when it was time. Until then, he continued to meet more clowns and take more pictures.

Popcorn was the next clown Marquis saw. Popcorn got his name from the popcorn popping machine that he pushes around plus he gives a bag of popcorn away to every little boy and girl.

"Popcorn! Popcorn, I want popcorn," Marquis exclaimed.

"Mom, may I have a bag, please?" he asked.

"It is free," said Popcorn the clown. Marquis' mom nods her head in agreement and smiles.

Popcorn said, "Here you go, and what is your name?"

"My name is Marquis. What is your name?" Marquis asked as he ate his popcorn.

The clown said, "My name is Popcorn,"

Marquis enjoyed meeting and talking with the clowns. Soon it was time for the show to start.

So, Marquis and his mom held hands and entered the Big Top. He was so excited!

Marquis and his mother took their seats on the first row. Marquis sat beside a little girl whose eyes were fixed with excitement as she held onto her chair and cotton candy, waiting for the show to begin.

Marquis turned to the little girl and said, "Hi, my name is Marquis. What is your name?"

The little girl answered Marquis without taking her eyes off the floor, "Michaela."

Marquis said, "I like the elephants and clowns. What do you like best?"

She turned and said, "I like the horses and when the people swing through the air. I want to join the circus when I grow up," Michaela exclaimed. Marquis thought that would be pretty neat! Because he wanted to ride the elephants.

The two children settled down in their seats as the show began.

They saw the elephants and the seals. Marquis and Michaela clapped and cheered.

Then came the horses and their riders. Michaela's eyes stretched wide, taking it all in. She even pretended she was riding on a horse.

There was a band, balloons, and acrobats. Oh, what fun they were having. It was a sight to behold.

"When will the clowns be coming out? Marquis asked his mother.

"They will be out at the end." she replied.

Michaela was so excited to see the people swinging and flipping in the air from one end of the tent to the other.

Michaela clapped her hands and said to her mother, "That is what I want to be when I grow up!" Michaela's mother just looked at her and smiled.

Now it was time for the clowns. They came out in a small car. Some were in the car and some were on top of the car.

The clowns were all different sizes. Some were tall, some short, some thin, and some were fat. There were silly clowns running all around, making jokes and falling down.

Marquis saw all the clowns he had taken pictures with earlier.

Trickster went to Marquis. Marquis became so excited because he knew Trickster was coming to get him to help with the balloon trick.

"Are you ready Little Man? It is time to do my surprise trick with the balloons."

"Yes, I am!" Marquis cheered.

No one knew that some of the balloons were filled with confetti and other prizes. So as the two of them tossed the balloons around in the crowd, Trickster would pick a girl or boy to throw balloons to, and when they were caught, the balloons would burst, and out came the confetti. There were also special balloons with a toy inside.

Marquis was having such a great time! He was tossing one balloon after the other.

"Look at me mom! I am helping Trickster," he shouted.

She smiled and waved at him. "I am so proud of you Marquis. You are doing a great job," she replied.

All the balloons were finally gone, and the show ended.

Trickster thanked Marquis and gave him a balloon and a top hat for helping him with his trick.

"Oh boy! Thank you, Mr. Trickster. Thank you!" Marquis politely shouted. He gave the clown the biggest hug.

Now, it was time to leave. Marquis had the best time ever. He met a new friend, Michaela, took pictures with lots of clowns from the show, and he got to help with the balloon trick.

"Thanks mom! This was the best time I have ever had. I will put away my toys, eat my vegetables, brush my teeth, and wash behind my ears from now on."

Marquis wrapped his arms around his mom's neck and gave her a big hug and kiss as she smiled proudly.

About the Author

Mary J. Bryant is an inspirational and children's author. She was inspired by her youngest son to write the first book, Marquis Finds a Friend. This series of books are called Marquis Adventures.

Marquis Goes to the Circus is the second book in the series. She hopes to inspire children to enjoy reading while enforcing those little life's lessons along the way.

Mary is married to Michael and they have three wonderfully talented children (Michael, Megan, Marquis). They also have a precious granddaughter (Michaela Jayne Grace).

More can be learned about the author and her books at www.doveministry378.org.

www.ingramcontent.com/pod-product-compliance
Lightning Source LLC
Chambersburg PA
CBHW042348300426
44110CB00032B/67